muffins

muffins
Sweet & Savory Comfort Food

cyndi duncan and georgie patrick

PHOTOGRAPHS BY JOYCE OUDKERK POOL

Gibbs Smith, Publisher
TO ENRICH AND INSPIRE HUMANKIND
Salt Lake City | Charleston | Santa Fe | Santa Barbara

First Edition
12 11 10 09 08   10 9 8 7 6 5 4 3 2 1

Published by
Gibbs Smith, Publisher
P.O. Box 667
Layton, Utah 84041

Orders: 1.800.835.4993
www.gibbs-smith.com

Printed and bound in China

Library of Congress Cataloging-in-Publication Data
Duncan, Cyndi.
  Muffins : sweet and savory comfort food / Cyndi Duncan and Georgie Patrick. — 1st ed.
    p. cm.
  ISBN-13: 978-1-4236-0188-3
  ISBN-10: 1-4236-0188-2
 1. Muffins. I. Patrick, Georgie. II. Title.

TX770.M83D845 2008
641.8'15—dc22
                     2007035082

To our mothers, Geneva Hewitt and Lucille Morrison,
the inspiring cooks in our lives,
and to our families for their love, support,
enthusiasm and unfailing belief in us
and our abilities to write cookbooks.

contents

acknowledgments

WE HAVE HAD MANY challenging experiences throughout our years of writing and publishing cookbooks, but we can say that it has been a truly rewarding experience as it has given us the opportunity to work together and with such wonderful people. Among the many we wish to thank are the following:

Georgie's mother, Geneva Hewitt, for kitchen testing our recipes in Texas; John and Charles Derick and the patrons of JD's Restaurant; Claudine Morgan and staff at The Guarantee Bank in Gatesville, Texas; the District IV employees at the Colorado State Highway Department; Drs. Cooper and Kaplan and staff; the people at the Windsor Center; our families and friends for tasting our many muffins, both successes and failures.

Those who sent us recipes to be tested and included in this cookbook.

The staff at the Tattered Cover Book Store for their encouragement during our "great muffin project."

Our families, L.G, Bob, Heidi, Wade, Toni, Wendi, Shawn and Heather, for "enjoying" muffins for breakfast, lunch, dinner, snacks, picnics, etc.

Photographer Joyce Oudkerk Pool, who turned an ordinary muffin cookbook into a work of art.

Editor Michelle Branson, for her support and tremendous enthusiasm for this project. And to the great staff at Gibbs Smith, Publisher, for believing in our muffin cookbook and working with us to complete it.

introduction

FOLLOWING THE SUCCESS of our first book, *Colorado Cookie Collection,* a friend at the Tattered Cover Bookstore in Denver suggested we write a muffin book. It wasn't until after agreeing to write the book that we realized the only thing we knew about muffins was how much we loved them. With the help of friends and families, we spent a year researching, experimenting with and tasting hundreds of muffins until we came up with the best. After a recipe was selected it was sent to Texas to be tested in home kitchens at a lower altitude. Fortunately, we found that altitude had little effect on our recipes if the oven was pre-heated and adjustment was made in cooking time (see Helpful Hints, page 13). From these we selected a variety of recipes for you that are not only easy to make, but also taste delicious.

During this "great muffin project" we came to the realization that in many ways our approach to baking differed. Mother Earth, Cyndi, cooks from scratch and is one of those incredibly organized cooks who does those wonderfully domesticated things in the kitchen. She is the one who grows her own fruits and vegetables, always has cookies in the cookie jar, and can feed an army of teenagers in fifteen minutes. Georgie, the Queen of Easy, who thinks of herself as an "efficient assembler" when it comes to cooking, buys most everything canned, sliced, diced and shredded from the grocery store. She thinks it helps the economy and, most importantly, leaves time for curling up with a good book.

In spite of our differences, we found that both of us have a real desire to write cookbooks that are used, not just shelved.

We wanted *Muffins* to be one of those books. Sitting at the kitchen table one afternoon, we outlined the features necessary for a great, easy-to-use cookbook for the Cyndis and Georgies of the world. It didn't take long to decide that a cookbook, to be well used, must have recipes with the most basic instructions and ingredients, include baking tips, appeal to the new cook as well as to the most experienced, and look fantastic. What better cookbook than *Muffins*?

We feel that the collection of recipes we ultimately included in *Muffins* and the format we chose to use have made this muffin book one of a kind. Not only is it a wonderful addition to your own cookbook library, it also makes an excellent gift for any Cyndi or Georgie.

Enjoy your *Muffins* and happy baking!

helpful hints

substitutions we found useful

- Replace buttermilk by souring 1 cup milk with 1 tablespoon lemon juice or white vinegar.
- Buttermilk and sour cream are interchangeable.
- Egg substitutes can be used in place of eggs. The package will state equivalents. Eggs and egg substitutes should be used at or close to room temperature.
- Interchange ingredients; e.g., apricots for peaches, dried cranberries for dried cherries, honey for 1/2 the molasses, light brown sugar for dark brown sugar (the difference is the amount of molasses mixed with sugar).
- For cream-style corn, substitute whole kernel corn plus 1/2 cup milk, buttermilk or plain yogurt. Add a pinch of baking soda.
- For fewer calories, use vegetable spray.
- Using oil in place of shortening in equal amounts is a matter of preference. With all the hoopla about trans fats, we generally substitute oil in most of our baking.
- Decreasing or omitting salt in recipes is okay. Salt is a flavor enhancer, but isn't always healthy.
- Sugar substitutes can replace equal amounts of granulated sugar; however, we have found that using equal amounts makes muffins too sweet so we cut the amount by 1/3. Baked products won't brown as well with sugar substitutes.

- Oats and quick oats can be interchanged. Old-fashioned or steel-ground oats may make the product grainier.
- Using more mashed ripe bananas in a recipe is okay without changing the end product too much. Muffins will be moister and heavier. Ripe bananas can be frozen until ready to use. When slightly thawed, they are easy to remove from the peel.

- Make your own oat bran by pulsing regular oats in a food processor until finely ground.
- Muffin recipe batter can be baked in loaf pans to make quick bread if desired. Longer baking time is required.
- Additions to sweet muffins: baking chips, fruits, dried fruits, nuts, extracts or liqueurs, spices.
- Additions to savory muffins: hard cheeses, mustards, herbs, hot pepper sauce, Worcestershire sauce, chopped vegetables, nuts or seeds.

baking tips

- Preheating the oven is necessary for muffins to rise properly.
- Muffin tins come in a variety of sizes. Adjust baking time accordingly.

- If one or two muffin cups are not filled with batter, fill 1/2 full with water for more even baking.
- Paper liners can be used rather than spraying cups with nonstick cooking spray.
- Muffin cups filled 2/3 full will have a flatter top; muffin cups filled 3/4 full will be more rounded and require slightly more baking time.
- Baking times vary with different ovens and locations. Adjust baking time accordingly.
- Check muffins close to end of stated baking time. When making miniature muffins, cut baking time in half.
- Note that convection ovens take less time for baking because of circulating air. For example, a convection oven setting at 325 degrees F equals the standard oven setting of 350 degrees F.

- Mixing a small amount of flour or powdered sugar with berries or nuts prevents them from sinking to the bottom.
- When muffins are done, they will spring back when touched; a toothpick inserted in the center will come out clean and they will be lightly browned.
- Muffins will be easier to remove if they are left in the pan for 4–5 minutes before removing them to a rack to cool. If necessary, loosen edges of muffins with a knife.

other tidbits

- Sifting flour is no longer necessary. Simply measure and combine dry ingredients.
- Usually stir wet ingredients into dry ingredients until just moistened. The

key to a good muffin texture is not to over stir the batter.

- Butter should be at room temperature or softened in the microwave for about 5–10 seconds.
- Most muffins can be frozen for a short period of time; wad up a piece of barely damp paper towel and lay on top of muffins inside the container. This keeps the muffins from taking on so much of a freezer taste.
- Toast sesame seeds or nuts in a skillet sprayed with nonstick cooking spray, stirring often and watching carefully as process goes quickly once heated.
- Dip measuring spoon in oil or cup of hot water before measuring honey, molasses or corn syrup to prevent sticking.

fiber

golden bran

GOLDEN RAISINS ADD WONDERFUL FLAVOR AND TEXTURE TO THESE FIBER-FILLED MUFFINS. THEY ARE DELICIOUS WITH A DOLLOP OF HONEY BUTTER.

1 cup buttermilk

2 slightly beaten eggs

1/4 cup melted and cooled, lightly salted butter or margarine

1/4 cup oil

2 1/2 tablespoons honey

1 1/2 tablespoons molasses

1 1/2 cups crumbled bran flakes

1/2 cup unprocessed bran

1 cup whole wheat flour

1/4 cup firmly packed dark brown sugar

1 teaspoon baking powder

1 teaspoon baking soda

1/4 teaspoon salt

3/4 cup golden raisins

Preheat oven to 400 degrees F. Spray muffin cups with nonstick cooking spray.

In large bowl, stir together buttermilk, eggs, butter, oil, honey and molasses until blended. Stir in bran flakes and bran, and let stand 1–2 minutes, or until cereal is softened.

In large bowl, stir flour, brown sugar, baking powder, baking soda and salt. Make a well in the center. Add bran mixture and stir just to combine. Stir in raisins.

Fill muffin cups 3/4 full. Bake for 15–20 minutes. Cool 5 minutes. Serve warm. Makes 12 muffins.

note: *Store in airtight container at room temperature 2–3 days. These muffins freeze well.*

carrot bran

CYNDI'S FAVORITE: SHE IS USUALLY A CHOCOLATE LOVER, BUT SHE REALLY APPRECIATES THE SPICY, MOIST, WHOLE GRAIN TEXTURE OF THESE MUFFINS.

3 cups flour
1 teaspoon baking soda
2 teaspoons baking powder
1/2 teaspoon salt, optional
1 tablespoon cinnamon
2 cups crumbled bran flakes
4 eggs
1 1/2 cups oil
1 1/4 cups firmly packed
   dark brown sugar
1/4 cup molasses
3 cups finely grated carrots
1 cup raisins or currants

Preheat oven to 350 degrees F. Spray muffin cups with nonstick cooking spray.

In large bowl, combine flour, baking soda, baking powder, salt and cinnamon; add bran and set aside.

In another large bowl, beat eggs, oil, brown sugar and molasses; stir in carrots and raisins. Combine egg and flour mixtures, stirring until just moist.

Fill muffin cups 3/4 full. Bake for 20 minutes. Makes 24 muffins.

variation: *For a different taste treat, use light brown sugar, substitute honey for ½ of the molasses and add nuts.*

banana bran

DO YOU ALWAYS HAVE ONE BANANA LEFT THAT TURNS BLACK? FREEZE IT EACH TIME, AND WHEN YOU HAVE ENOUGH, THAW AND BAKE SOMETHING YUMMY.

1 1/3 cups all bran cereal
1 cup mashed banana
6 tablespoons oil
1/3 cup honey
1/4 cup molasses
1 egg, room temperature
1 teaspoon fresh lemon juice
1 cup plus 2 tablespoons flour
1 1/4 teaspoons baking powder
1/2 teaspoon cinnamon
1 teaspoon baking soda
1/2 teaspoon salt, optional
1/2 cup chopped dates, optional

Preheat oven to 400 degrees F. Spray muffin cups with nonstick cooking spray.

Mix first 7 ingredients in medium bowl.

Combine flour, baking powder, cinnamon, baking soda and salt in large bowl. Stir in dates.

Make well in center of dry ingredients. Add banana mixture to well and stir until just blended. Batter will be lumpy.

Fill muffin cups 3/4 full. Bake for 15–20 minutes. Cool 5 minutes; remove from pan. Makes 12 muffins.

easy bran

THE BRAN FLAKES IN THESE MUFFINS ARE CRUNCHY WHEN FIRST BAKED, BUT BECOME CHEWY WHEN REHEATED. THEY TASTE GREAT BOTH WAYS.

2 tablespoons shortening
3 tablespoons sugar
1 egg
3/4 cup milk
1 cup bran flakes
1 cup flour
2 teaspoons baking powder
1/2 teaspoon salt, optional

Preheat oven to 375 degrees F. Spray muffin cups with nonstick cooking spray.

Cream shortening and sugar in large bowl until light and fluffy. Add egg and beat well.

Stir in milk, add bran flakes and mix well.

In small bowl, combine flour, baking powder and salt, and stir into bran mixture just until moistened.

Fill muffin cups 2/3 full. Bake for 20–25 minutes. Makes 12 muffins.

light bran

THE COMBINATION OF WHEAT AND OAT BRAN GIVES THESE MUFFINS A DELICATE TEXTURE; GREAT SERVED AT BREAKFAST WITH HONEY BUTTER.

2 large eggs
1/4 cup firmly packed
  light brown sugar
1 cup milk
1/4 cup oil
1 1/2 cups wheat bran cereal
1/2 cup oat bran
1/2 cup flour
2 teaspoons baking powder

Heat oven to 375 degrees F. Spray muffin cups with nonstick cooking spray.

Beat eggs and brown sugar in medium bowl until smooth. Whisk in milk and oil. Stir in wheat bran cereal. Let stand at least 10 minutes.

Combine oat bran, flour and baking powder in large bowl. Add wheat bran mixture and stir just until dry ingredients are moistened.

Fill muffin cups 3/4 full. Bake 20–25 minutes, or until brown and firm in the center. Makes 12 muffins.

variation: *Brush muffins with maple syrup when removed from oven; or add 1/2 cup raisins or 1/2 cup walnuts to batter before baking.*

cheddar bran

SERVE THESE MUFFINS WARM WITH HERBED BUTTER TO BEST EXPERIENCE THE CHEDDAR FLAVOR.

1 cup whole bran
1 1/4 cups buttermilk or
  sour milk
1/4 cup shortening
1/3 cup sugar
1 egg
1 1/2 cups flour
1 1/2 teaspoons baking powder
1/2 teaspoon salt, optional
1/4 teaspoon baking soda
1 cup shredded sharp cheddar
  cheese

Preheat oven to 400 degrees F. Spray muffin cups with nonstick cooking spray.

In small bowl, soften bran in buttermilk. In large bowl, cream shortening and sugar until fluffy. Beat in egg.

In separate bowl, combine flour, baking powder, salt and baking soda. Add to creamed mixture alternately with bran mixture. Stir in cheese.

Fill muffin cups 2/3 full. Bake for 15–20 minutes. Makes 12 muffins.

honey bran

A HEALTHY CHOICE MADE EVEN HEALTHIER WHEN SALT IS OMITTED AND HONEY, EGG SUBSTITUTE, SUNFLOWER OIL AND HARD RED SPRING WHEAT BRAN IS USED.

1 cup boiling water

1 cup raisins or chopped dates

2 1/2 teaspoons baking soda

1 1/2 cups honey or 1 cup sugar

2 3/4 cups flour

1/2 teaspoon salt, optional

2 eggs

1/2 cup oil

2 cups buttermilk

3 to 4 cups unprocessed wheat bran

Preheat oven to 375 degrees F. Spray muffin cups with nonstick cooking spray.

Pour boiling water over dates or raisins and add baking soda. Lightly mix remaining ingredients together in a separate bowl. Add date mixture; stir until just moistened.

Fill muffin cups 3/4 full. Bake for 20 minutes. Makes 12 muffins.

whole wheat bran

BET YOU CAN'T EAT JUST ONE OF THESE WONDERFULLY MOIST
BRAN MUFFINS.

3 cups crumbled bran flakes

1/2 cup oil

1 cup raisins

1 cup boiling water

2 eggs, lightly beaten

2 cups buttermilk

1/4 cup molasses

2 1/4 cups whole wheat flour

4 teaspoons sugar

2 1/2 teaspoons baking soda

1/4 teaspoon salt, optional

Preheat oven to 400 degrees F. Spray muffin cups with nonstick cooking spray.

Combine bran flakes, oil and raisins in large bowl and pour the boiling water over them. Set mixture aside to cool.

Combine eggs, buttermilk and molasses in small bowl. Add to cereal mixture.

Combine flour, sugar, baking soda and salt in another small bowl and add to cereal mixture. Stir only enough to moisten dry ingredients. Cover and let stand at least 15 minutes; 1 hour is preferred.

Fill muffin cups 3/4 full. Bake for 15–20 minutes. Makes 24 muffins.

rosemary carrot

THE ROSEMARY IN THIS MUFFIN RECIPE MAKES IT QUITE UNUSUAL. THE COMBINATION OF SLIGHTLY SWEET CURRANTS AND THE HERB FLAVOR IS DELIGHTFUL.

1 cup currants
1 1/2 cups boiling water
1/2 cup olive oil
1/2 teaspoon vanilla
2 cups flour
1 cup whole wheat flour
2/3 cup sugar
2 teaspoons baking soda
2 teaspoons crushed rosemary
2 cups grated carrots

Preheat oven to 375 degrees F. Spray muffin cups with nonstick cooking spray.

In small bowl, combine currants, boiling water, olive oil and vanilla; set aside.

In large bowl, combine flours, sugar, baking soda and rosemary. Make well in center of dry ingredients. Add wet ingredients, stirring until moistened. Fold in carrots until evenly blended.

Fill muffin cups 2/3 full. Bake for 20–25 minutes. Makes 12 muffins.

whole wheat

FOR AN EVEN HEALTHIER MUFFIN, USE EGG SUBSTITUTE AND REDUCE OR OMIT SALT.

2 cups whole wheat flour
2 tablespoons brown sugar
2 teaspoons baking powder
1 1/2 teaspoons ground cinnamon
1/4 teaspoon salt
1 egg, beaten
1 cup plus 2 tablespoons
   skim milk
3 tablespoons melted butter

Preheat oven to 400 degrees F. Spray muffin cups with nonstick cooking spray.

Combine first five ingredients in large bowl; make a well in center of mixture.

Whisk egg, milk and butter in small bowl; add to dry ingredients, stirring just until moistened.

Fill muffin cups 2/3 full. Bake for 15–20 minutes. Makes 12 muffins.

fruit

true-blue berry

1/4 cup butter, melted
1/2 cup sugar
1 egg
1 1/4 cups flour
2 teaspoons baking powder
1/2 teaspoon salt, optional
1/4 cup milk
3/4 cup canned blueberries,
    drained but not rinsed,
    saving 1/4 cup juice

Preheat oven to 400 degrees F. Spray muffin cups with nonstick cooking spray.

Cream butter, sugar and egg in large bowl.

Combine flour, baking powder and salt in medium bowl.

Stir flour mixture into creamed mixture alternately with milk and juice from blueberries. Fold in blueberries.

Fill muffin cups 2/3 full. Bake for 20 minutes. Makes 12 muffins.

blueberry pinwheel

THIS MUFFIN TAKES A LITTLE MORE TIME TO PREPARE, BUT THE END PRODUCT IS LOVELY. MMMM GOOD FOR BREAKFAST, LUNCH OR DINNER.

2 cups biscuit mix

2 tablespoons sugar

2/3 cup milk

2 tablespoons grated orange peel

1/4 cup melted butter

1 can (15 ounces) blueberries, drained

1/2 teaspoon ground cinnamon

1/3 cup chopped nuts

1/3 cup firmly packed brown sugar

Preheat oven to 425 degrees F. Spray muffin cups with nonstick cooking spray.

Combine biscuit mix and sugar. Stir in milk and orange peel just until moistened.

Knead about ten times on floured surface, until dough is smooth. Roll out to 10 x 18-inch oblong. Brush dough with melted butter. Sprinkle remaining ingredients over dough.

Roll up jelly roll fashion starting at the 18-inch side. Cut roll into 12 equal pieces and place in muffin cups.

Bake for 15–20 minutes. Makes 12 muffins.

saucy blueberry lemon

THESE WONDERFULLY TART CREATIONS MELT IN YOUR MOUTH.

1/2 cup butter or margarine
1/2 cup sugar
2 eggs
2 cups flour
3 teaspoons baking powder
1/4 teaspoon salt, optional
1/3 cup milk
1 cup canned or thawed and
   drained frozen blueberries
Rind of one lemon, finely grated

sauce:
1/4 cup fresh lemon juice
1/3 cup sugar

Preheat oven to 350 degrees F. Spray muffin cups with nonstick cooking spray.

Cream butter, sugar and eggs in a small bowl.

In large bowl, combine flour, baking powder and salt. Add creamed mixture alternately with milk until mixed. Fold in blueberries and lemon rind.

Fill muffin cups 2/3 full. Bake for 25–30 minutes.

For the sauce, combine lemon juice and sugar in small pan and bring to a boil.

Pour sauce evenly over top of hot muffins. Makes 12 muffins.

state fair blueberry

THESE PRIZEWINNING MUFFINS ARE REGULARS AT STATE FAIR COMPETITIONS.

1/4 cup shortening

1 cup sugar

2 eggs

1 cup milk

1 teaspoon baking soda

2 1/2 cups flour

2 teaspoons cream of tartar

1/4 teaspoon salt, optional

1 1/2 cups rinsed and drained
   blueberries

Preheat oven to 350 degrees F. Spray muffin cups with nonstick cooking spray.

Cream shortening and sugar; add eggs and milk.

Combine dry ingredients in separate bowl; add to creamed mixture just until moistened. Fold in blueberries

Fill muffin cups 2/3 full. Bake for 20–25 minutes. Makes 12 muffins.

crunchy apple

THIS APPLE MUFFIN RECIPE MAKES GREAT MUFFIN TOPS.

1 cup sugar
1/2 cup oil
2 eggs
1 teaspoon vanilla
1 1/2 cups flour
1 teaspoon baking soda
1/2 teaspoon apple pie spice
2 cups grated apples
1/2 cup chopped walnuts,
   optional
1/2 cup raisins, optional

crunch topping:
1/4 cup butter
1/2 cup flour
3 tablespoons sugar

Preheat oven to 350 degrees F. Spray muffin cups with nonstick cooking spray.

Cream sugar, oil, eggs and vanilla in small bowl.

Mix together flour, baking soda and apple pie spice in large bowl. Add creamed mixture, stirring just until moistened. Fold in apples, nuts and raisins.

Fill muffin cups 2/3 full.

For crunch topping, mix butter, flour and sugar with fork or pastry blender in medium bowl. Spoon evenly over batter in muffin cups.

Bake for 25–30 minutes. Makes 12 muffins.

spicy peach nut

APRICOTS CAN BE SUBSTITUTED FOR PEACHES IN THIS DELIGHTFULLY LIGHT-TEXTURED MUFFIN.

1 can (15 ounces) peaches, drained
  and chopped; reserve juice
Buttermilk
2 1/2 cups flour
1 1/2 cups sugar
1 teaspoon baking powder
1 1/2 teaspoons baking soda
1/2 teaspoon nutmeg
1/2 teaspoon cloves
1/2 teaspoon ginger
1 teaspoon cinnamon
3 tablespoons butter, melted
  and cooled
2 eggs

glaze:
4 tablespoons reserved peach juice
1 cup powdered sugar
1/2 cup chopped walnuts

Preheat oven to 350 degrees F. Spray muffin cups with nonstick cooking spray.

Measure 4 tablespoons reserved peach juice into small bowl and set aside.

Add buttermilk to remaining reserved peach juice to equal 1 cup.

Combine dry ingredients in large bowl.

In medium bowl, combine butter and eggs. Stir in buttermilk mixture. Fold peaches into egg mixture. Mix egg mixture with dry ingredients just until moistened.

Fill muffin cups 2/3 full. Bake for 20–25 minutes.

For the glaze, mix together reserved peach juice, powdered sugar and nuts. Spread glaze evenly over warm muffins. Makes 18 muffins.

41

blueberry oatmeal

OATS MAKE THIS MUFFIN MORE TEXTURED, SPICES MAKE IT MORE FLAVORFUL, AND BUTTERMILK TAKES IT UP A NOTCH.

1 cup firmly packed light
 brown sugar
1/4 cup unsalted butter
1 egg
1 1/8 cups quick oats
1 cup buttermilk
1 tablespoon vanilla
1 1/4 cups flour
1 tablespoon baking powder
1 teaspoon salt
1 teaspoon cinnamon
1/2 teaspoon baking soda
1/2 teaspoon nutmeg
1/2 cup finely chopped walnuts
1 1/3 cups fresh blueberries

Preheat oven to 400 degrees F. Spray muffin cups with nonstick cooking spray.

In large bowl, cream brown sugar and butter. Add egg and beat well. Stir in oats, buttermilk and vanilla.

In large bowl, mix flour, baking powder, salt, cinnamon, baking soda, nutmeg and walnuts.

Add butter mixture, stirring just until moistened. Fold in blueberries.

Fill muffin cups 2/3 full. Bake for 15–20 minutes. Makes 18 muffins.

oatmeal apple raisin

THESE MUFFINS ARE VERY COARSELY TEXTURED AND TASTY.

1 egg

3/4 cup milk

1 cup raisins

1 chopped apple

1/2 cup oil

1 cup whole wheat flour

1 cup quick oats

1/4 cup sugar

2 teaspoons baking powder

1 teaspoon salt, optional

1 teaspoon nutmeg

2 teaspoons cinnamon

Preheat oven to 400 degrees F. Spray muffin cups with nonstick cooking spray.

In large bowl, beat egg. Add remaining ingredients until just moistened.

Fill muffin cups 3/4 full. Bake for 15–20 minutes. Makes 12 muffins.

tangy lemon

THESE MUFFINS ARE REMINISCENT OF TANGY LEMON SQUARES.

1 3/4 cups flour
3/4 cup sugar
1 tablespoon grated lemon peel
1 teaspoon baking powder
3/4 teaspoon baking soda
1/4 teaspoon salt
1 container (8 ounces) lemon
    yogurt
6 tablespoons butter, melted
    and cooled
1 egg, room temperature
1 tablespoon fresh lemon juice

glaze:
1/3 cup fresh lemon juice
1/4 cup sugar
2 teaspoons grated lemon peel

note: *Serve at room temperature.*

Preheat oven to 400 degrees F. Spray muffin cups with nonstick cooking spray.

Mix first 6 ingredients in large bowl and make well in center.

Whisk yogurt, butter, egg and lemon juice in another bowl. Stir egg mixture into dry ingredients just until moistened.

Fill muffin cups 3/4 full. Bake for 20 minutes.

Meanwhile, cook glaze ingredients in non-aluminum saucepan over low heat until sugar dissolves.

Pierce each muffin 6–8 times with toothpick. Drizzle hot glaze over each muffin. Makes 12 muffins.

rum raisin

EVEN IF YOU'RE NOT FOND OF RUM, YOU'LL LOVE THESE. SOAKING THE RAISINS AND CURRANTS IN REAL RUM MAKES ALL THE DIFFERENCE.

1/2 cup golden raisins
1/2 cup dried currants
1/2 cup dark rum or 2 tablespoons
   rum extract plus 1/4 cup water
2 cups flour
3/4 cup sugar
1 1/2 teaspoons baking powder
1/2 teaspoon baking soda
1/4 teaspoon salt
1/4 teaspoon freshly ground nutmeg
6 tablespoons butter, softened
1 cup sour cream
1 egg, room temperature
3/4 teaspoon vanilla

glaze:
1/3 cup powdered sugar
Several drops fresh lemon juice

In small bowl, cover raisins and currants in rum and soak overnight, stirring occasionally.

Preheat oven to 400 degrees F. Spray muffin cups with nonstick cooking spray. Drain fruit, reserving rum.

Mix flour, sugar, baking powder, baking soda, salt and nutmeg in large bowl. Cut in butter until coarse meal forms. Mix in fruit.

In small bowl, whisk sour cream, egg, vanilla and 2 tablespoons reserved rum until smooth. Stir into flour mixture just until moistened.

Fill muffin cups 3/4 full. Bake for 15–20 minutes.

To make a thin glaze, combine powdered sugar and lemon juice together with about 1 tablespoon of reserved rum. Drizzle glaze over slightly cooled muffins. Makes 16 muffins.

apple carrot

THE GRANNY SMITH APPLES PROVIDE A NICE TARTNESS AND AN ATTRACTIVE COLOR COMBINATION WITH THE CARROTS.

2 eggs

3/4 cup sugar

1/4 cup oil

1/2 cup buttermilk or milk

2 cups chopped Granny Smith apples

1/2 cup shredded carrots

2 cups flour

2 teaspoons baking powder

1/2 teaspoon baking soda

1 teaspoon cinnamon

1/2 teaspoon salt, optional

Preheat oven to 350 degrees F. Spray muffin cups with nonstick cooking spray.

Combine eggs, sugar, oil and buttermilk in large bowl. Stir in apples and carrots.

Mix dry ingredients together in separate bowl. Combine with egg mixture, stirring just until moistened.

Fill muffin cups 2/3 full. Bake for 20–25 minutes. Makes 16 muffins.

spicy apple

THIS MUFFIN HAS A GENTLE TASTE OF SPICE CAKE THAT IS ENHANCED WHEN
SERVED WITH A TABLESPOON OF FRUIT PRESERVES.

1 2/3 cups flour

3 tablespoons sugar

2 1/2 teaspoons baking powder

1 teaspoon ground cinnamon

1/2 teaspoon ground nutmeg

1/4 teaspoon salt

1 egg, beaten

1 cup skim milk

2 tablespoons oil

1 cup finely chopped apple

Preheat oven to 400 degrees F. Spray muffin cups with nonstick cooking spray.

Combine flour, sugar, baking powder, cinnamon, nutmeg and salt in large bowl. Make a well in center of mixture.

In small bowl, combine egg, milk and oil; pour into center of dry ingredients, stirring just until moistened. Fold in apple.

Fill muffin cups 3/4 full. Bake for 15–20 minutes. Makes 12 muffins.

chocolate chip banana

THESE MUFFINS CAPTURE THE FLAVOR OF CHOCOLATE-COVERED BANANAS.

1/2 cup softened butter
1 cup firmly packed light
   brown sugar
2 eggs, lightly beaten
5 to 6 ripe bananas, mashed
2 cups flour
1/2 teaspoon salt
1/2 teaspoon baking powder
3/4 teaspoon baking soda
3/4 cup chopped nuts
3/4 cup mini chocolate chips

Preheat oven to 350 degrees F. Spray muffin cups with nonstick cooking spray.

In large bowl, cream together butter and brown sugar. Add eggs and bananas; mix well.

In separate bowl, combine flour with salt, baking powder and baking soda. Stir in creamed mixture just until moistened. Fold in nuts and chocolate chips.

Fill muffin cups 2/3 full. Bake for 20–25 minutes or until golden brown. Makes 12 muffins.

graham pear

GRAHAM CRACKERS ADD A FLAVORFUL TWIST TO A MUFFIN ALREADY FILLED WITH TASTY SURPRISES.

2 cans (16 ounces each) pears
1/2 cup graham cracker crumbs
4 1/2 cups flour
1 cup firmly packed brown sugar
4 teaspoons baking powder
1 teaspoon salt
2 teaspoons cinnamon
1 teaspoon baking soda
3/4 teaspoon ground allspice
1 cup margarine
2 cups light sour cream
4 large eggs
2/3 cup sliced almonds

streusel topping:
4 tablespoons flour
1/4 cup firmly packed
  brown sugar
2 tablespoons graham cracker crumbs
2 tablespoons margarine
1/2 teaspoon cinnamon

Preheat oven to 350 degrees F. Spray muffin cups with nonstick cooking spray.

Drain pears and pat dry with paper towel. Chop coarsely.

In large bowl, stir dry ingredients until well mixed. Cut in margarine until crumbly.

In medium bowl, whisk sour cream and eggs. Fold egg mixture, pears and almonds into dry ingredients. Fill muffin cups 3/4 full.

Mix streusel topping ingredients in small bowl; sprinkle evenly over batter. Bake for 25–30 minutes. Makes 24 muffins.

apple surprise

TRY MIXING THE INGREDIENTS ALL TOGETHER FOR A YUMMY TASTE—LIKE A CHOCOLATE-COVERED APPLE FROM THE CANDY STORE.

2 medium apples, peeled, cored
*   and diced*
1/2 teaspoon cinnamon
1 tablespoon sugar
1/4 cup chopped nuts
1/4 cup melted butter
1/4 cup unsweetened cocoa
3/4 cup applesauce
1 1/4 cups flour
1/2 cup sugar
3/4 teaspoon baking soda
1/4 teaspoon salt
1 egg, slightly beaten

Preheat oven to 375 degrees F. Spray muffin cups with nonstick cooking spray.

Combine apples, cinnamon, 1 tablespoon sugar and nuts in small bowl; mix well and set aside.

Thoroughly combine butter and cocoa; add applesauce.

In large bowl, combine flour, 1/2 cup sugar, baking soda and salt. Stir in cocoa mixture and egg just until moistened.

Place 1 tablespoon batter in each of 12 muffin cups; spoon 1 heaping tablespoon apple mixture into each cup, pressing into batter. Cover each cup with 1 tablespoon batter.

Bake for 15–20 minutes. Makes 12 muffins.

honey oat apple

WHEAT GERM MAKES THIS MUFFIN A HEALTHIER TREAT FOR A MID-MORNING PICK-ME-UP.

3/4 cup milk

1 egg

1/4 cup oil

1/4 cup honey

1 cup rolled oats

1 cup whole wheat flour

1/2 cup chopped apple

1/3 cup wheat germ

1/4 cup firmly packed
   brown sugar

1 tablespoon baking powder

3/4 teaspoon cinnamon

1/4 teaspoon salt, optional

Preheat oven to 400 degrees F. Spray muffin cups with nonstick cooking spray.

In large bowl, mix milk, egg, oil and honey thoroughly. Add other ingredients, mixing just until moistened.

Fill muffin cups 2/3 full. Bake for 15–20 minutes. Makes 12 muffins.

blackberry

WHAT CAN YOU SAY EXCEPT "GIVE ME ANOTHER ONE, PLEASE!" THOSE BIG BLACKBERRIES ARE IRRESISTIBLE.

1/2 cup butter
1 container (6 ounces)
   blackberry yogurt
1/2 cup sugar
2 eggs
3 1/2 cups flour, divided
2 teaspoons baking powder
1 teaspoon baking soda
1/2 teaspoon salt
1 cup buttermilk
1/2 cup skim milk
1 teaspoon vanilla
1 package (16 ounces) frozen
   blackberries, thawed

topping:
1/2 cup sliced almonds
2 to 3 tablespoons buttermilk
1/4 cup sugar
Pinch of cinnamon

Preheat oven to 400 degrees F. Spray muffin cups with nonstick cooking spray.

In large bowl, cream butter with yogurt, sugar and eggs. In separate bowl, combine all but 3 tablespoons flour, baking powder, baking soda and salt.

Combine milks and vanilla in a small bowl. Alternately add milk and flour mixtures to egg mixture.

In large bowl, sprinkle reserved flour over berries and gently fold into batter. Fill each muffin cup 3/4 full.

For topping, combine ingredients and spoon evenly over batter.

Bake 15–20 minutes. Makes 24 muffins.

note: *Best when served warm. Refrigerate or freeze leftover muffins. They ferment quickly.*

56

miniature orange

MAKE THESE MINIATURES FOR A GREAT ADDITION TO ANY BRUNCH MENU. THESE BITE-SIZED MORSELS ARE EASY FOR CHILDREN TO HOLD AND EAT.

2 cups sugar, divided
1/2 cup orange juice
1/2 cup butter
2 cups flour
1 teaspoon baking soda
1 teaspoon salt
1 cup sour cream
1 teaspoon grated orange rind
1/2 cup raisins
1/2 cup chopped nuts

Preheat oven to 375 degrees F. Spray miniature muffin cups with nonstick cooking spray.

In small bowl, mix 1 cup sugar and orange juice. Set aside for dipping after muffins are baked.

In large bowl, cream butter and 1 cup sugar.

In medium bowl, combine flour, baking soda, and salt. Add sour cream alternately with the dry ingredients to the butter mixture until just moistened. Fold in orange rind, raisins and nuts. (The batter will be stiff.)

Fill muffins cups 3/4 full. Bake for 10–12 minutes.

While still warm, dip muffins in the sugar–orange juice mixture. Makes about 36 miniature muffins.

ginger orange

AAH, A SOOTHING TASTE OF GINGER IS GOOD FOR THE MIND AND SOUL.

3/4 cup flour
3/4 cup whole wheat flour
2/3 cup sugar
1 1/4 teaspoons ground ginger
2 teaspoons baking powder
1/2 teaspoon baking soda
1/4 teaspoon salt
1 tablespoon grated orange peel
7 tablespoons butter, melted and
   cooled to lukewarm
1/3 cup sour cream
1/3 cup fresh orange juice
2 eggs, room temperature

Preheat oven to 400 degrees F. Spray muffin cups with nonstick cooking spray.

Mix first 7 ingredients in large bowl. Stir in orange peel.

Whisk butter, sour cream, orange juice and eggs in a medium bowl.

Make well in center of dry ingredients. Add butter mixture; stir until just blended (batter will be lumpy).

Fill muffin cups 3/4 full. Bake for 15–20 minutes. Makes 12 muffins.

orange blossom

1/4 cup sugar
1 tablespoon flour
1/2 teaspoon cinnamon
1/4 teaspoon nutmeg
1 tablespoon margarine
1 egg, slightly beaten
1/2 cup orange juice
1/2 cup orange marmalade
2 cups prepared biscuit mix
1/4 cup chopped pecans

Preheat oven to 400 degrees F. Spray muffin cups with nonstick cooking spray.

In small bowl, combine sugar, flour, cinnamon and nutmeg. Cut in margarine until crumbly. Set aside.

Combine egg, juice and marmalade in medium bowl. Add biscuit mix. Stir vigorously for 30 seconds. Stir in nuts.

Fill muffin cups 1/2 full. Sprinkle crumbly mixture over batter. Bake for 15–20 minutes. Makes 12 muffins.

rhubarb

THESE MUFFINS ARE ANOTHER FAVORITE OF CYNDI'S. DON'T LIMIT THE USE OF RHUBARB TO SPRING; IT IS AVAILABLE IN THE GROCER'S FROZEN-FOOD SECTION.

1 1/2 cups firmly packed
   brown sugar
1/2 cup oil
1 egg
1 teaspoon vanilla
1 cup buttermilk
1/2 cup chopped walnuts or
   pecans
2 1/2 cups flour
1 teaspoon baking soda
1 teaspoon baking powder
1/2 teaspoon salt
1 1/2 cups diced rhubarb
Sugar

Preheat oven to 350 degrees F. Spray muffin cups with nonstick cooking spray.

In large bowl, mix together brown sugar, oil, egg and vanilla until well blended.

Add remaining ingredients except rhubarb and mix until moistened. Fold in rhubarb.

Fill muffin cups 2/3 full. Sprinkle a pinch or two of sugar on top of batter.

Bake for 20–25 minutes. Makes 12 muffins.

buttermilk apple

3/4 cup firmly packed
  brown sugar
1/3 cup oil
1 egg, slightly beaten
1 teaspoon vanilla
1 1/2 cups flour
1/2 teaspoon baking soda
1/4 teaspoon salt
1 cup peeled and chopped apple
1/2 cup buttermilk

topping:
1/4 cup firmly packed
  brown sugar
1/4 cup chopped pecans
1/2 teaspoon cinnamon

Preheat oven to 325 degrees F. Spray muffin cups with nonstick cooking spray.

Blend brown sugar, oil, egg and vanilla in large bowl.

In medium bowl, combine flour, baking soda and salt; add to wet mixture. Stir in apple and buttermilk, and mix thoroughly just to moisten.

Fill muffin cups 2/3 full.

For the topping, combine 1/4 cup brown sugar, pecans and cinnamon in small bowl. Sprinkle evenly over batter.

Bake for 20–25 minutes. Makes 12 muffins.

banana streusel

IF YOU LIKE BANANAS, YOU'LL LOVE THESE MUFFINS. THIS RECIPE IS ONE OF CYNDI'S FAVORITES TO MAKE INTO A LOAF BREAD.

2 cups flour

1/4 cup sugar

1/4 cup firmly packed brown sugar

2 teaspoons baking powder

1/2 teaspoon baking soda

1/2 teaspoon salt, optional

1/2 teaspoon cinnamon

1/4 teaspoon nutmeg

3 ripe bananas, mashed

1/2 cup buttermilk

1/3 cup oil

1 egg

1/4 cup chopped pecans, optional

streusel topping:

3 tablespoons butter

1/2 cup flour

3 tablespoons sugar

Preheat oven to 375 degrees F. Spray muffin cups with nonstick cooking spray.

In large mixing bowl, combine flour, sugars, baking powder, baking soda, salt, cinnamon and nutmeg.

In a separate bowl, combine banana, buttermilk, oil, egg and pecans. Stir into flour mixture until just moistened.

Fill muffin cups 2/3 full.

For streusel topping, cut 3 tablespoons butter into 1/2 cup flour and 3 tablespoons sugar in small bowl. Sprinkle mixture over the batter.

Bake for 15–20 minutes. Makes 12 muffins.

pineapple coconut

THE FULL CREAMY FLAVOR OF PIÑA COLADA CAN BE ENJOYED IN THESE BEAUTIFULLY LIGHT-TEXTURED MUFFINS.

1 yellow cake mix

1 cup water

1/4 cup butter, melted and cooled

2 eggs, beaten

*1 can (8 ounces) crushed
   pineapple, drained, reserving
   3 tablespoons juice*

2/3 cup flaked coconut

topping:

1/3 cup flaked coconut

3 tablespoons pineapple juice

3/4 cup powdered sugar

Preheat oven to 350 degrees F. Spray muffin cups with nonstick cooking spray.

In large bowl, combine cake mix, water, butter, eggs, pineapple and coconut. Mix thoroughly, but do not beat.

Fill muffin tins 3/4 full. Bake 25–30 minutes. Turn oven to broil.

Mix topping ingredients in small bowl. Spoon mixture evenly over muffins.

Broil 1–2 minutes just until coconut topping is slightly bubbly. Makes 24 muffins.

orange crunch

THE CEREAL NUGGETS GIVE THIS MUFFIN ITS NUTTY CRUNCH.

2 cups flour

1/3 cup sugar

1 teaspoon baking powder

1/2 teaspoon baking soda

3/4 teaspoon salt, optional

1/2 cup malted cereal nuggets

2 eggs, well beaten

1 tablespoon grated orange peel

1 cup orange juice

1/3 cup oil

Preheat oven to 400 degrees F. Spray muffin cups with nonstick cooking spray.

Combine the first five ingredients.

In large bowl, mix remaining ingredients. Add flour mixture; stir just until moistened.

Fill muffin cups 2/3 full. Bake for 15–20 minutes. Makes 14–16 muffins.

tropical fruit

ALTHOUGH PASSION FRUIT JUICE AND GUAVA JELLY ARE SOMETIMES DIFFICULT TO LOCATE, THESE MUFFINS MAKE THE SEARCH WORTH THE EFFORT.

1 package dry active yeast

1/4 cup very warm water
  (105 to 115 degrees F)

1/2 cup cooked and mashed
  sweet potato

1/4 cup butter, softened

1/2 cup sugar

3/4 teaspoon salt

1/2 cup warm passion fruit juice

1 egg, beaten

2 cups flour

1/4 cup drained crushed
  pineapple

1/3 cup guava jelly

Preheat oven to 375 degrees F. Spray muffin cups with nonstick cooking spray.

Dissolve yeast in water.

Beat sweet potato and butter in large bowl. Add sugar and salt. Beat two minutes.

Add juice, egg and yeast mixture; beat one minute. Stir in flour just until moistened. Fold in pineapple.

Fill muffin cups 2/3 full. Let rise just to the tops of the cups—about 45 minutes.

Spoon about 1 teaspoon of jelly on center of each muffin.

Bake for 20 minutes or until golden brown. Makes 18 muffins.

cranberry maple

IN THE SUMMER WHEN FRESH CRANBERRIES AREN'T PLENTIFUL, USE A CAN
OF WHOLE CRANBERRY SAUCE AND REDUCE THE SUGAR TO ½ CUP.

2 cups flour

1/2 cup chopped walnuts

2 teaspoons baking powder

1/2 teaspoon baking soda

1/2 teaspoon salt

1 1/2 cups sliced or chopped
   cranberries

1/2 cup unsalted butter, softened

2 eggs

1 cup sugar

2/3 cup buttermilk

2 teaspoons maple flavoring

Preheat oven to 350 degrees F. Spray muffin cups with nonstick cooking spray.

In large bowl, mix flour, walnuts, baking powder, baking soda and salt. Stir in cranberries.

In separate bowl, beat together butter, eggs, sugar, buttermilk and maple flavoring. Stir into dry ingredients just until moistened.

Fill muffin cups 2/3 full. Bake for 20–25 minutes. Makes 12 muffins.

granny's cranberry

USE DRIED OR FROZEN CRANBERRIES IF FRESH CRANBERRIES ARE NOT AVAILABLE.

3/4 cup halved cranberries
1/2 cup powdered sugar
2 cups flour
3 teaspoons baking powder
1/2 teaspoon salt
1/4 cup sugar
1 egg, well beaten
1 cup milk
4 tablespoons shortening, melted

Preheat oven to 375 degrees F. Spray muffin cups with nonstick cooking spray.

In small bowl, mix cranberries with powdered sugar.

In large bowl, combine dry ingredients. Stir in egg, milk and shortening all at once. Fold in cranberries.

Fill muffins cups 2/3 full. Bake for 20–25 minutes. Makes 12 muffins.

raspberry

1 1/2 cups flour

1/2 teaspoon baking soda

1/2 teaspoon salt

1 1/2 teaspoons cinnamon

1 cup sugar

2 eggs, well beaten

2/3 cup oil

1 package (12 ounces) frozen unsweetened raspberries, thawed

1/2 cup chopped pecans

Preheat oven to 400 degrees F. Spray muffin cups with nonstick cooking spray.

In medium bowl, mix flour, baking soda, salt, cinnamon and sugar. Make well in center and stir in eggs and oil. Fold in undrained raspberries and pecans.

Fill muffin cups 2/3 full. Bake for 15–20 minutes. Makes 12 muffins.

raspberry wine

3 cups flour, divided
1 tablespoon baking powder
1/2 teaspoon salt, optional
1/8 teaspoon baking soda
1/2 cup butter or margarine
1 cup sugar
1 teaspoon vanilla
2 eggs
1/2 cup raspberry wine
1/2 cup water
1 cup coarsely chopped fresh or
   frozen raspberries

Preheat oven to 400 degrees F. Spray muffin cups with nonstick cooking spray.

Reserve 3 tablespoons flour in small bowl.

In large mixing bowl, stir together remaining flour, baking powder, salt and baking soda; set aside.

In separate mixing bowl, beat butter with electric mixer. Add sugar and vanilla, beating until smooth. Add eggs, one at a time, beating well.

Stir together wine and water. Add wine mixture and creamed mixture to flour mixture, stirring just until moistened. Toss together reserved flour and berries; gently fold into batter.

Fill muffin cups 2/3 full. Bake for 18–20 minutes. Makes 16–18 muffins.

cheery cherry

FOR A DIFFERENT CHERRY FLAVOR, SUBSTITUTE CHOPPED FRESH CHERRIES OR DRIED CHERRIES. CHERRY LOVERS WON'T STOP AT JUST ONE.

2 cups flour
1/3 cup sugar
1/3 cup quartered maraschino cherries
1 tablespoon baking powder
1/2 teaspoon salt, optional
3/4 cup buttermilk
1/4 cup oil
4 tablespoons cherry juice
1 egg, beaten
1 teaspoon almond extract

topping:
4 tablespoons finely chopped almonds
3 tablespoons sugar

Preheat oven to 350 degrees F. Spray muffin cups with nonstick cooking spray.

In large mixing bowl, combine flour, sugar, cherries, baking powder and salt.

In separate bowl, mix buttermilk, oil, cherry juice, egg and almond extract.

Make a well in dry ingredients and stir in liquid just to moisten.

Fill muffin cups 2/3 full.

For the topping, combine almonds and 3 tablespoons sugar, and sprinkle over batter. Bake for 20–25 minutes. Makes 12 muffins.

note: *Cool 10 minutes before removing from muffin cups.*

frosted pumpkin

THIS RECIPE IS A FALL FAVORITE THAT CAN BE ENJOYED ALL YEAR LONG, THANKS TO CANNED PUMPKIN. THESE MUFFINS TASTE LIKE OUR FAVORITE PUMPKIN BARS.

1 cup flour
1/2 cup sugar
2 teaspoons baking powder
1/2 teaspoon cinnamon
1/2 teaspoon nutmeg
1/4 teaspoon salt, optional
1/4 cup butter or margarine
1 egg, beaten
1/2 cup canned pumpkin
1/2 cup evaporated milk
1/2 cup seedless raisins

cream cheese frosting:
3 ounces cream cheese at room
   temperature
1/2 cup butter or margarine
2 tablespoons milk
1 teaspoon vanilla
2 cups powdered sugar

Preheat oven to 400 degrees F. Spray muffin cups with nonstick cooking spray.

Combine flour, sugar, baking powder, cinnamon, nutmeg and salt together in medium bowl. Cut in butter until mixture resembles cornmeal.

Combine egg with pumpkin and milk. Stir in raisins. Add egg mixture to dry ingredients, stirring just to moisten.

Fill muffin cups 2/3 full. Bake for 15–20 minutes. Cool.

In large bowl, beat frosting ingredients until smooth. Frost cooled muffins. Makes 16 muffins.

rich coffee date

BREAK TIME IS EXTRA SPECIAL WHEN SERVING THESE MUFFINS WITH HOT CHOCOLATE. THE COMBINATION CREATES A DELIGHTFUL MOCHA TASTE.

1 3/4 cups flour

2 1/2 teaspoons baking powder

1 cup water

1 egg

1/3 cup oil

1/4 cup sugar

1 1/2 teaspoons instant coffee powder (not freeze-dried)

3/4 teaspoon salt

1 package (8 ounces) pitted dates

Preheat oven to 400 degrees F. Spray muffin cups with nonstick cooking spray.

Mix flour and baking powder together in large mixing bowl.

Using a blender, mix water, egg, oil, sugar, instant coffee powder, salt and dates until dates are coarsely chopped. Pour date mixture over dry ingredients, stirring just until moistened.

Fill muffin cups 2/3 full. Bake for 15–20 minutes. Makes 12 muffins.

vegetable

zucchini nut

PUT THOSE EXTRA ZUCCHINI TO GOOD USE IN THESE MUFFINS AND FREEZE TO ENJOY IN THE OFF-SEASON.

2 eggs, slightly beaten
1/2 cup firmly packed
   brown sugar
1/2 cup honey
1/2 cup butter or margarine,
   melted
1 teaspoon vanilla
1 3/4 cups flour
1 teaspoon baking soda
1 teaspoon salt, optional
1/2 teaspoon baking powder
1/2 teaspoon ground nutmeg
1 1/2 teaspoons ground cinnamon
1 cup granola cereal
1/2 cup chopped walnuts
2 cups shredded zucchini

Preheat oven to 350 degrees F. Spray muffin cups with nonstick cooking spray.

In large bowl, beat eggs, brown sugar, honey, butter and vanilla.

In separate bowl, stir together the flour, baking soda, salt, baking powder, nutmeg and cinnamon.

Add dry ingredients to egg mixture, stirring just until moistened. Fold in granola, nuts and zucchini.

Fill muffin cups 3/4 full. Bake for 20–25 minutes. Makes 18 muffins.

zucchini oatmeal

THE OATMEAL AND PECANS GIVE THESE MUFFINS A NUTTY FLAVOR.

2 1/2 cups flour

1 1/2 cups sugar

1 cup chopped pecans

1/2 cup uncooked quick oats

1 tablespoon baking powder

1 teaspoon salt

1 teaspoon cinnamon

4 eggs, slightly beaten

1 medium zucchini, shredded,
   drained and liquid squeezed
   out

3/4 cup oil

Preheat oven to 400 degrees F. Spray minia-ture muffin cups with nonstick cooking spray.

In large bowl, mix first 7 ingredients. Mix in eggs, zucchini and oil just until moistened.

Fill muffin cups 2/3 full. Bake for 10–15 minutes. Makes 30–36 miniature muffins.

sweet potato

FRAGRANT WITH SPICES, THESE SPARK APPETITES FOR A HEARTY BREAKFAST OR DINNER.

1 1/2 cups flour
1/4 cup firmly packed light
  brown sugar
1 tablespoon baking powder
1/2 teaspoon salt
1/2 teaspoon ground cinnamon
1/4 teaspoon ground nutmeg
1 egg
1/2 cup milk
1 cup cooked and mashed
  sweet potatoes
1/4 cup butter, melted
1/2 cup raisins

Heat oven to 400 degrees F. Spray muffin cups with nonstick cooking spray.

In medium bowl, combine flour, brown sugar, baking powder, salt, cinnamon and nutmeg.

In small bowl, beat together egg, milk, sweet potatoes and butter. Add egg mixture to dry ingredients, stirring just until moistened. Stir in raisins.

Fill muffin cups 2/3 full. Bake for 15–20 minutes. Makes 12 muffins.

red and green bell pepper

THIS IS A GREAT-SMELLING COMPLEMENT TO HEARTY SOUPS.

1/2 cup butter

1/3 cup chopped green onion

1/3 cup finely chopped
red bell pepper

1/4 cup finely chopped
green bell pepper

2/3 cup sour cream

2 eggs

1 1/2 cups flour

2 tablespoons sugar

2 teaspoons baking powder

3/4 teaspoon salt

1/2 teaspoon baking soda

1/2 teaspoon dried basil

1/4 teaspoon dried tarragon

Preheat oven to 400 degrees F. Spray muffin cups with nonstick cooking spray.

Melt butter in skillet with onion and peppers; cook until tender, about 7 minutes, stirring often. Cool to lukewarm.

Whisk sour cream and eggs in medium bowl. Stir in cooled onion mixture.

Combine flour, sugar, baking powder, salt, baking soda and herbs in large bowl; make well in center. Add sour cream mixture, stirring just until blended.

Fill muffin cups 3/4 full. Bake for 15–20 minutes. Makes 10 muffins.

mushroom

FOR THOSE WHO LOVE MUSHROOMS, THIS MUFFIN IS BEST WHEN SERVED WARM WITH A SALAD OR BOWL OF SOUP.

1 can (4 ounces) mushrooms,
  stems and pieces, or 1 cup
  fresh, sliced mushrooms and
  increase milk to 1 cup
1 tablespoon butter
2 cups flour
1/4 cup sugar
3 teaspoons baking powder
1 teaspoon salt
l egg
3/4 cup milk
1/2 cup grated white cheddar
  cheese
1/4 cup oil

Preheat oven to 400 degrees F. Spray muffin cups with nonstick cooking spray.

Drain mushrooms; reserve 1/4 cup liquid. Sauté mushrooms in butter.

In large bowl, combine dry ingredients.

In small bowl, beat egg slightly with a fork; stir in mushroom liquid and milk. Stir in cheese, mushrooms and oil. Add to dry ingredients and stir just until moistened.

Fill muffin cups 2/3 full. Bake for 15–20 minutes. Makes 12–16 muffins.

creamy corn

THIS IS A TRUE CORNY CORN MUFFIN FOR WHOLE WHEAT LOVERS.

1 cup whole wheat flour

1 cup yellow cornmeal

4 teaspoons baking powder

1/2 teaspoon salt, optional

1/4 cup sugar

2 eggs, slightly beaten

1 cup skim milk

2 tablespoons butter or
   margarine, melted

1 cup cream style corn

Preheat oven to 400 degrees F. Spray muffin cups with nonstick cooking spray.

Combine flour, cornmeal, baking powder, salt and sugar in large bowl.

In smaller bowl, beat together eggs, milk, butter and corn. Add egg mixture to flour mixture, stirring only until moistened.

Fill muffin cups 2/3 full. Bake for 15–20 minutes. Makes 12 muffins.

jalapeño corn

GREAT WITH BUTTER. FOR A TWIST, MIX THE JALAPEÑO JELLY INTO THE BATTER—MAKES A TOTALLY DIFFERENT MUFFIN.

1 cup flour
1 cup yellow cornmeal
1/4 cup sugar
1 tablespoon baking powder
1/2 teaspoon salt
1 teaspoon crushed
   red pepper flakes
1 egg
1/2 cup plus 1 teaspoon milk
1/4 cup corn oil
1/2 cup shredded cheddar cheese
1 can (17 ounces) cream style
   corn
1/4 cup mild jalapeño pepper
   jelly

Preheat oven to 375 degrees F. Spray muffin cups with nonstick cooking spray.

In large bowl, mix together flour, cornmeal, sugar, baking powder, salt and pepper flakes.

Whisk together egg, milk, oil, cheese and corn in small bowl. Pour liquid mixture over dry ingredients, stirring just until moistened.

Fill muffin cups 1/2 full. Reserve 1/3 batter. With back of teaspoon, make a small depression in center of each muffin and drop in 1 teaspoon jalapeño jelly. Spoon reserved batter evenly over jelly.

Bake for 15–20 minutes. Makes 12 muffins.

cornbread

1 cup yellow cornmeal
1 cup flour
3 tablespoons sugar
Pinch of salt
4 teaspoons baking powder
4 tablespoons butter, melted
1 cup milk
1 egg, slightly beaten

Preheat oven to 400 degrees F. Spray muffin cups with nonstick cooking spray.

In large bowl, mix together cornmeal, flour, sugar, salt and baking powder. Add butter, milk and egg; stirring until moistened.

Fill muffin cups 3/4 full. Bake for 10–12 minutes. Makes 12 muffins.

quick corn

A CHEESY TASTE HIGHLIGHTS THIS QUICK AND EASY CORN MUFFIN RECIPE.

1 package (14 ounces) corn
    muffin mix
1 can (8 3/4 ounces) cream style
    corn
1 egg, slightly beaten
1/2 cup shredded American
    cheese
Dash hot pepper sauce

Preheat oven to 400 degrees F. Spray muffin cups with nonstick cooking spray.

Combine all ingredients in large bowl, mixing just until blended.

Fill muffin cups 2/3 full. Bake for 12–15 minutes. Makes 10–12 muffins.

bacon chive corn

THESE MUFFINS MAKE A TASTY ADDITION TO A HOT BOWL OF BEAN SOUP ON A COLD WINTER NIGHT.

1 package (14 ounces)
corn muffin mix
2 teaspoons snipped chives
Dash of pepper
6 slices bacon, crisp cooked,
drained and crumbled

Preheat oven to 400 degrees F. Spray muffin cups with nonstick cooking spray.

Prepare muffin mix according to package directions. Fold in chives, pepper and bacon.

Fill muffin cup 2/3 full. Bake for 15–17 minutes. Makes 12 muffins.

favorites

p. b. and j.

2 cups flour
1/2 cup sugar
2 1/2 teaspoons baking powder
1/2 teaspoon salt
1/2 cup chunky peanut butter
2 tablespoons butter or
    margarine
1 cup milk
2 eggs, well beaten
1/4 cup currant jelly, or jelly of
    your choice, melted
1/2 cup finely chopped peanuts

Preheat oven to 400 degrees F. Spray muffin cups with nonstick cooking spray.

Combine flour, sugar, baking powder and salt in large bowl. Cut in peanut butter and butter until mixture resembles coarse crumbs. Add milk and eggs all at once, stirring just until moistened.

Fill muffin cups 2/3 full. Bake for 15–17 minutes.

Remove from tins and immediately brush with melted jelly. Dip in chopped peanuts. Makes 18 muffins.

breakfast

THESE MUFFINS HAVE THE SPICY AND SUGARY TASTE OF DOUGHNUTS. USE MINIATURE MUFFIN PANS FOR A RESEMBLANCE TO DOUGHNUT HOLES.

1 1/2 cups plus 2 tablespoons
   flour
3/4 cup sugar
2 teaspoons baking powder
1/4 teaspoon salt
2/3 teaspoon nutmeg
1/2 cup milk
1 egg, beaten
2/3 cup butter, melted and
   divided

topping:
1/2 cup sugar
1 teaspoon cinnamon
1/2 teaspoon vanilla

Preheat oven to 400 degrees F. Spray muffin cups with nonstick cooking spray.

In large bowl, combine first five ingredients. Add milk, egg and 1/3 cup melted butter. Mix thoroughly.

Fill muffin cups 1/2 full. Bake for 20 minutes or until lightly browned.

While baking, mix topping ingredients in a small bowl.

Remove muffins from tin immediately, dip in remaining 1/3 cup melted butter and roll in topping mixture. Makes 12 muffins.

pound cake

TASTY JUST PLAIN, BUT EVEN TASTIER SERVED WITH FRESH FRUIT AND CREAM.

1 3/4 cups flour
1/2 teaspoon salt
3/4 teaspoon baking soda
3/4 cup sugar
1/2 cup lightly salted butter,
    softened
1/2 cup sour cream
1 teaspoon vanilla
1/2 teaspoon lemon juice
2 eggs

Preheat oven to 350 degrees F. Spray muffin cups with nonstick cooking spray.

In small bowl, mix together flour, salt and baking soda.

In large bowl, beat sugar and butter until fluffy. Beat in sour cream, vanilla and lemon juice. Beat in eggs, one at a time. Stir in dry ingredients just until moistened.

Fill muffin cups 2/3 full. Bake for 20–25 minutes. Makes 12 muffins.

poppy seed coffee cake

THESE ARE ABSOLUTELY DELICIOUS AND ARE GEORGIE'S FAVORITE POPPY SEED MUFFINS.

1/4 cup poppy seeds
1 cup buttermilk
1 teaspoon almond extract
1 cup butter
1 1/2 cups sugar
4 eggs, separated
2 1/2 cups flour
1 teaspoon baking powder
1 teaspoon baking soda
1/2 cup sugar
1 teaspoon cinnamon

Preheat oven to 350 degrees F. Spray muffin cups with nonstick cooking spray.

In large bowl, combine poppy seeds, buttermilk and almond extract; set aside. In small bowl, cream butter and sugar. Add egg yolks and beat. Combine buttermilk and creamed mixtures.

In another large bowl, combine the flour, baking powder and baking soda; add to buttermilk mixture just until moistened. In a separate bowl, beat egg whites until stiff. Fold into flour mixture. Fill muffin cups 1/3 full.

Mix together 1/2 cup sugar and 1 teaspoon cinnamon; sprinkle half of mixture evenly over batter. Divide remaining batter into muffin cups. Sprinkle remaining sugar-cinnamon mixture over batter. Cut through each cup with knife to create a marbled effect.

Bake for 20–25 minutes. Makes 30 muffins.

orange poppy seed

THESE MUFFINS ARE DELIGHTFULLY DIFFERENT WITH A HINT OF ORANGE AND NUTMEG.

3/4 cup sugar
1/4 cup butter, softened
1/2 teaspoon grated orange peel
2 eggs
2 cups flour
2 1/2 teaspoons baking powder
1/2 teaspoon salt
1/4 teaspoon nutmeg
1 cup milk
1/4 cup golden raisins
1/2 cup chopped pecans
5 tablespoons poppy seeds

Preheat oven to 400 degrees F. Spray muffin cups with nonstick cooking spray.

In large bowl, cream sugar, butter and orange peel. Add eggs, one at a time, beating well after each.

Combine flour, baking powder, salt and nutmeg in medium bowl. Add to creamed mixture alternately with milk, beating well after each addition. Fold in raisins, nuts and poppy seeds.

Fill muffin cups 3/4 full. Bake 15–20 minutes, or until lightly browned. Makes 12 muffins.

maple pecan

THESE ARE WONDERFULLY CAKE-LIKE MUFFINS THAT ARE CHUNKY WITH PECANS.

1 1/2 cups flour
2 teaspoons baking powder
1/4 teaspoon salt
1/4 teaspoon allspice
1 3/4 cups coarsely chopped
   toasted pecans
1/2 cup firmly packed dark
   brown sugar
1/2 cup butter, melted
1/3 cup milk
1/4 cup maple syrup
1 egg
1 teaspoon vanilla

Preheat oven to 400 degrees F. Generously spray muffin cups with nonstick cooking spray.

Mix flour, baking powder, salt and allspice in large bowl. Stir in pecans.

Whisk brown sugar, butter, milk, syrup, egg and vanilla in medium bowl.

Make well in center of dry ingredients. Add butter mixture to well; stir into dry ingredients until just moistened.

Fill muffin cups 3/4 full. Bake for 15–20 minutes, or until golden brown. Makes 12 muffins.

walnut streusel

3 cups flour, divided
1 1/2 cups firmly packed
  brown sugar
3/4 cup butter or margarine
1 cup chopped walnuts, divided
2 teaspoons baking powder
1/2 teaspoon nutmeg
1/2 teaspoon ginger
1/2 teaspoon baking soda
1/2 teaspoon salt
1 cup buttermilk or sour milk
2 eggs, beaten

Preheat oven to 350 degrees F. Spray muffin cups with nonstick cooking spray.

In medium bowl, combine 2 cups flour and brown sugar. Cut in butter to make fine crumbs.

In small bowl, combine 3/4 cup of the crumbs and 1/4 cup of the walnuts; set aside.

Into remaining crumb mixture, stir in remaining 1 cup flour, baking powder, spices, baking soda, salt and remaining 3/4 cup walnuts.

In another small bowl, combine buttermilk and eggs; stir into dry ingredients just to moisten. Fill muffin cups 2/3 full. Top each with a generous spoonful of reserved crumb nut mixture.

Bake for 20–25 minutes or until springy to the touch. Makes 18 muffins.

coffee cake

THESE TASTY TREATS ARE SUPERB FOR A COFFEE BREAK, SERVED WARM OR COLD. AS A QUICK ALTERNATIVE, BAKE IN 9 x 13-INCH BAKING DISH.

2 1/4 cups flour

1 cup sugar

1/2 cup butter or margarine

1 egg

1 cup buttermilk

1 1/2 teaspoons baking soda

1/2 cup chopped walnuts or
    pecans

1/2 cup raisins

Preheat oven to 375 degrees F. Spray muffin cups with nonstick cooking spray.

In large bowl, combine flour and sugar. Melt butter and pour over flour mixture, mixing until crumbly. Set aside 1 cup of mixture for topping.

Add the rest of the ingredients to the remainder of flour mixture, stirring just until moistened. (Batter will be thin and lumpy.)

Fill muffin cups 3/4 full. Sprinkle reserved mixture over top of each muffin. Bake for 15–20 minutes. Makes 12 muffins.

spice cake

THESE MUFFINS ARE A REAL HIT WHEN SERVED WITH PUMPKIN MOUSSE.

1/4 cup shortening
1/4 cup sugar
1 egg
1/2 cup molasses
1 1/2 cups flour
3/4 teaspoon baking soda
1/4 teaspoon salt
1/2 teaspoon cinnamon
1/2 teaspoon ginger
1/4 teaspoon cloves
1/2 cup hot water

Preheat oven to 375 degrees F. Spray muffin cups with nonstick cooking spray.

In large bowl, cream together shortening and sugar. Beat in egg and molasses.

In large bowl, combine flour, baking soda, salt, cinnamon, ginger and cloves.

Stir into molasses mixture. Gradually add hot water, mixing until moistened.

Fill muffin cups 2/3 full. Bake for 15–20 minutes. Makes 12 muffins.

surprise

2 cups flour
1/4 cup sugar
1 teaspoon baking powder
1/2 teaspoon baking soda
1/4 teaspoon salt
1/4 cup butter, melted
1 cup plain yogurt
1/4 cup milk
1 egg
1/2 teaspoon vanilla
1/4 cup jam or preserves
Powdered sugar, optional

Preheat oven to 400 degrees F. Spray muffin cups with nonstick cooking spray.

In large bowl, mix flour, sugar, baking powder, baking soda and salt, stirring until well blended.

Pour butter into small mixing bowl. Add yogurt and milk, stirring until smooth. Beat in egg and vanilla. Add butter mixture to dry ingredients, stirring until moistened.

Fill muffin cups 1/2 full. Spoon 1 teaspoon jam on batter in each cup. Top with remaining batter.

Bake for 15–20 minutes. Let stand 5 minutes, remove to rack and sift powdered sugar over each muffin before serving, if desired. Makes 12 muffins.

quick sesame cheese

TRY MIXING THE SESAME SEEDS INTO BATTER FOR A MORE DISTINCT SESAME FLAVOR.

2 tablespoons sesame seeds
1/2 cup minced onion
2 tablespoons butter
3 cups biscuit mix
1 1/2 cups grated sharp
   cheddar cheese, divided
2 eggs, well beaten
1 cup milk

Preheat oven to 400 degrees F. Spray muffin cups with nonstick cooking spray.

Toast sesame seeds in small frying pan over medium heat until lightly browned. Set aside to cool.

In another small frying pan, sauté onions in butter until transparent.

In large bowl, stir biscuit mix and 1 cup cheese together.

In small bowl, combine egg, milk and onion; add to cheese mixture and mix vigorously for 30 seconds.

Fill muffin cups 2/3 full. Sprinkle tops with remaining cheese and the sesame seeds.

Bake for 15–20 minutes. Makes about 15 muffins.

cheddar rye

This is a flavorful, heavier muffin that is very tasty with potato soup or a sauerkraut dish.

1/2 cup flour

1/2 cup rye flour

3 tablespoons sugar

2 teaspoons baking powder

1 teaspoon caraway seed

1/2 teaspoon baking soda

1/2 teaspoon salt

1 2/3 cups finely grated
   extra-sharp cheddar cheese

6 tablespoons oil

2/3 cup sour cream

1/2 cup milk

1 egg, room temperature

1 teaspoon Worcestershire sauce

Preheat oven to 400 degrees F. Spray muffin cups with nonstick cooking spray.

Mix first 7 ingredients in large bowl. Stir cheese into dry ingredients.

Whisk oil, sour cream, milk, egg and Worcestershire sauce in medium bowl until smooth. Add sour cream mixture to dry ingredients, stirring just until moistened.

Fill muffin cups 3/4 full. Bake for 15–20 minutes. Makes 12 muffins.

double fudge

LIKE BROWNIES, THESE ARE DEFINITELY FOR THE CHOCOLATE CONNOISSEURS.

5 ounces coarsely chopped
    semisweet chocolate
2 ounces coarsely chopped
    unsweetened chocolate
1/3 cup butter
3/4 cup sour cream
2/3 cup firmly packed
    brown sugar
1/4 cup light corn syrup
1 egg
1 1/4 teaspoons vanilla
1 1/2 cups flour
1 teaspoon baking soda
1/4 teaspoon salt
5 ounces semisweet chocolate,
    cut into 1/3-inch pieces or
    1 cup semisweet chocolate chips

Preheat oven to 400 degrees F. Spray muffin cups with nonstick cooking spray.

Melt first 3 ingredients in medium bowl in microwave or in a double boiler. Stir until smooth. Cool slightly. Whisk sour cream, brown sugar, corn syrup, egg and vanilla into chocolate.

Mix flour, baking soda and salt in large bowl. Mix in chopped chocolate or chips. Make well in center of dry ingredients.

Add chocolate mixture to well; stir into dry ingredients until just moistened.

Fill muffin cups 3/4 full. Bake for 15–20 minutes. Makes 16 muffins.

pizza

A MUFFIN OF A DIFFERENT FLAVOR. SERVE WARM WITH SALAD OR CHEESE.

2 cups flour

1/4 cup grated Parmesan cheese

1 tablespoon sugar

2 teaspoons baking powder

1/2 teaspoon baking soda

1/4 teaspoon cayenne pepper

1/4 cup chopped pimiento-
stuffed green olives

1/4 cup finely chopped tomato

1 1/2 teaspoons Italian
seasoning mix

1 medium garlic clove, minced

2 eggs

1/2 cup olive oil

1/3 cup milk

1/3 cup sour cream

Preheat oven to 400 degrees F. Spray muffin cups with nonstick cooking spray.

Mix first 6 ingredients in large bowl. Stir in olives, tomato, Italian seasoning and garlic.

In small bowl, whisk eggs, then oil, milk and sour cream. Add to flour mixture, stirring until moistened.

Fill muffin cups 3/4 full. Bake for 15–20 minutes or until golden brown. Makes 12 muffins.

bacon cornettes

AN EXCELLENT CORNMEAL MUFFIN FOR THE BACON LOVER.

10 to 12 slices bacon
1 cup flour
1/4 cup sugar
4 teaspoons baking powder
3/4 teaspoon salt
1 cup yellow cornmeal
2 eggs, well beaten
1 cup milk
1/4 cup oil

Preheat oven to 425 degrees F. Spray muffin cups with nonstick cooking spray.

Cook bacon until crisp; drain and crumble.

In large bowl, combine next 4 ingredients; stir in cornmeal. Add eggs, milk and oil. Mix just until moistened. Stir in bacon. If desired, save some crumbs for the top of the muffins.

Fill muffin cups 2/3 full. Bake for 15–20 minutes. Makes 12 muffins.

dijon ham

A HEARTY MUFFIN FOR A HEARTY SOUP. YOU WILL LOVE THE MUSTARDY HAM FLAVOR.

1 2/3 cups flour

1/3 cup white cornmeal

1/4 cup sugar

2 teaspoons dry mustard

1 1/2 teaspoons baking powder

3/4 teaspoon salt

1/2 teaspoon baking soda

1/8 teaspoon freshly ground
  pepper

1/8 teaspoon cloves

1 1/4 cups finely chopped
  smoked ham

2 eggs

1 cup buttermilk

1/3 cup oil

3 tablespoons Dijon mustard

Preheat oven to 400 degrees F. Spray muffin cups with nonstick cooking spray.

Mix first 9 ingredients in large bowl. Stir in ham.

Whisk eggs in medium bowl to blend. Whisk buttermilk, oil and mustard into eggs.

Make well in center of dry ingredients; add buttermilk mixture, stirring just until moistened. Fill muffin cups 3/4 full.

Bake for 15–20 minutes. Makes 12–14 muffins.

dilly

CYNDI BAKES THIS RECIPE IN A ROUND DISH TO SERVE AS A BREAD ON
SPECIAL OCCASIONS.

1 packet yeast

1/4 cup warm water

1 cup cottage cheese, heated to
   lukewarm

2 tablespoons sugar

1 tablespoon minced onion

1 tablespoon butter

2 teaspoons dill seed

1 teaspoon salt

1/4 teaspoon baking soda

1 egg

2 1/4 to 2 1/2 cups flour

Heat oven to 350 degrees F. Spray muffin
cups with nonstick cooking spray.

Soften yeast in warm water.

Combine remaining ingredients and add
yeast mixture. Stir just until moistened.

Fill muffin cups 1/2 full. Let rise 30 minutes.

Bake for 15–20 minutes. Makes 12 muffins.

cheese caraway

THESE CHEESY MUFFINS HAVE A LIGHTER RYE TASTE THAT COMPLEMENTS HEAVIER SOUPS.

1 3/4 cups flour

1/4 cup sugar

2 1/2 teaspoons baking powder

3/4 teaspoon salt

2 teaspoons caraway seeds

1 egg, well beaten

1/3 cup oil

1 cup milk

1/2 cup grated sharp processed
   American cheese

1/2 cup grated Swiss cheese

Preheat oven to 350 degrees F. Spray muffin cups with nonstick cooking spray.

Combine dry ingredients in large bowl.

In small bowl, combine egg, oil and milk. Mix into dry ingredients just until moistened. Fold in cheeses.

Fill muffin cups 2/3 full. Bake for 15–20 minutes. Makes 12 muffins.

cream cheese

THIS IS OUR VERSION OF THE DELICIOUS CREAM CHEESE MUFFINS WE'VE ALL HAD AT OUR FAVORITE BREAKFAST HANGOUTS.

2 cups flour

3/4 cup plus 3 tablespoons
   sugar, divided

1 1/2 teaspoons baking powder

1/2 teaspoon baking soda

6 tablespoons butter, cut up

1 cup buttermilk

3 tablespoons orange juice

1 tablespoon grated orange peel

1 egg

4 ounces cream cheese, cut into
   12 cubes

streusel topping:

1/3 cup flour

3 tablespoons sugar

1 tablespoon orange juice

2 tablespoons butter, softened

Preheat oven to 400 degrees F. Spray muffin cups with nonstick cooking spray.

In medium bowl, combine flour, 3/4 cup sugar, baking powder and baking soda. With pastry blender or fork, cut in butter until mixture is crumbly.

In small bowl, whisk buttermilk, orange juice, orange peel and egg together. Stir buttermilk mixture into dry ingredients just until moistened.

Fill muffin cups 3/4 full. Dip each cube of cream cheese into the remaining 3 tablespoons sugar and press into batter.

In small bowl, mix streusel ingredients until crumbly. Spread evenly among muffin cups. Bake for 15–20 minutes. Makes 12 muffins.

note: *Store in refrigerator.*

spicy chocolate

A current trend of blending chile, cinnamon and chocolate gives this muffin an unusual flair.

2 cups flour
1/2 cup sugar
1/2 cup firmly packed
    brown sugar
1/4 cup cocoa
2 teaspoons baking powder
1 teaspoon instant coffee
1 teaspoon chile powder
3/4 teaspoon cinnamon
2 eggs
1 cup milk
1 tablespoon vinegar
1/3 cup butter, melted
1 teaspoon vanilla

topping:
3 tablespoons sugar
1 1/2 teaspoons chile powder

Preheat oven to 400 degrees F. Spray muffin cups with nonstick cooking spray.

In large bowl, combine flour, sugars, cocoa, baking powder, instant coffee, chile powder and cinnamon.

In medium bowl, whisk eggs, milk, vinegar, butter and vanilla. Stir into dry ingredients just until moistened. Fill muffin tins 3/4 full.

For topping, combine sugar and chile powder in small bowl. Sprinkle topping mixture on batter.

Bake for 15–20 minutes. Makes 12 muffins.

index

Metric Conversion Chart

Liquid and Dry Measures

U.S.	Canadian	Australian
¼ teaspoon	1 mL	1 ml
½ teaspoon	2 mL	2 ml
1 teaspoon	5 mL	5 ml
1 tablespoon	15 mL	20 ml
¼ cup	50 mL	60 ml
⅓ cup	75 mL	80 ml
½ cup	125 mL	125 ml
⅔ cup	150 mL	170 ml
¾ cup	175 mL	190 ml
1 cup	250 mL	250 ml
1 quart	1 liter	1 litre

Temperature Conversion Chart

Fahrenheit	Celsius
250	120
275	140
300	150
325	160
350	180
375	190
400	200
425	220
450	230
475	240
500	260